20th Century Inventions
FILM AND TELEVISION

Louise Wordsworth

RAINTREE
STECK-VAUGHN
PUBLISHERS
The Steck-Vaughn Company

Austin, Texas

ST. AGNES / ST. DOMINIC LIBRARY

026975

20th Century Inventions

AIRCRAFT

CARS

COMPUTERS

DIGITAL REVOLUTION

FILM AND TELEVISION

THE INTERNET

LASERS

MEDICAL ADVANCES

NUCLEAR POWER

ROCKETS AND SPACECRAFT

SATELLITES

TELECOMMUNICATIONS

Front cover and title page: A mixing desk in a television editing room
Back cover and contents page: A television camera films a tennis match.

© Copyright 1999, text, Steck-Vaughn Company

Published by Raintree Steck-Vaughn Publishers, an imprint of Steck-Vaughn Company

Library of Congress Cataloging-in-Publication Data
Wordsworth, Louise.
Film and television / Louise Wordsworth.
        p.   cm.—(20th century inventions)
        Includes bibliographical references and index.
        Summary: Describes the past, present, and possible
        future of the film and television industries.
        ISBN 0-8172-4898-6
        1. Motion pictures—Juvenile literature.
        2. Television broadcasting—Juvenile literature.
        [1. Motion pictures. 2. Television broadcasting.]
        I. Title. II Series.
        PN1994.W664   1998
        791.43—dc21   97-41560

Printed in Italy. Bound in the United States.
1 2 3 4 5 6 7 8 9 0 01 00 99 98 97

Picture acknowledgments
Mary Evans 6; Eye Ubiquitous 41/David Cummings; Getty Images 13; Ronald Grant Archive 16/David James, 18/Richard Foreman, 19/Richard Foreman, 28, 29/Frank Masi, 30/Walt Disney Co, 31, 33; Image Bank 5/David W. Hamilton; NMPFT/Science & Society Picture Library 7, 9, 10, 14, 44 (right); Pictor 40; Science Photo Library *cover & title page/* Phil Jude, *back cover & contents page/*Philippe Plailly, 8, 22 (top)/James Stevenson, 22 (lower)/Adam Hart-Davies, 24/Adam Hart-Davies, 32/Philippe Plailly, 36/Geoff Tompkinson, 37 (lower)/David Parker, 42/James King-Holmes & W Industries, 43/Will & Demi McIntyre, 44 (left); Sony 39; Topham 15, 45 (top); Wayland Picture Library 4/Rupert Horrox, 11/Rupert Horrox, 21/Rupert Horrox, 27 (lower)/Zak Waters, 34/Zak Waters, 35/Zak Waters, 45 (right)/Rupert Horrox; Zefa 22/ J. Maher, 27(top)/Damm, 37 (top). Artwork is by Tim Benké.

CONTENTS

MOVING PICTURES

Film and television have an amazing impact on our daily lives, yet film has been available for only a century, and television is an even more recent invention. Many technological advances have taken place since an audience first sat down to watch a motion picture, but throughout all those years film and television have never failed to fascinate people all over the world.

More than 500 million households in the world have at least one television set, while over 300 million households have two or more. Children in the United States and United Kingdom spend an average of three to four hours a day watching television. A blockbuster movie can attract approximately 15 percent of the population into theaters. Could you imagine life without movies and television? How would people spend their free time?

Teenagers all over the world enjoy a visit to the movies.

Some people argue that we have come to rely on film and television too much and point out that there are better ways of spending our free time. This may be true, but it could also be argued that film and television provide us with a great deal of information and enjoyment.

Today, we take films and television programs for granted. Yet most of us know little of how the special effects, color, sound, and other features are created and put together. This book will look at the story of movies and television and at how they have developed into the twentieth century's most popular forms of entertainment.

Television is the world's most popular form of entertainment—and can be enjoyed by the whole family. In 1995, 98 percent of American households had at least one TV set, and 81 percent also had VCRs.

The first cinemas

The very first films were shown in theaters, stores, or even tents. But by the early twentieth century, the demand to watch moving pictures was so great that special buildings in which to show them had to be constructed. In 1905, cinemas called nickelodeons opened in the United States. The name came about because people paid a nickel to see a movie.

THE STORY OF MOVIES

A magic lantern show from the 1880s. Shows like these had thrilled audiences for more than two centuries.

The development of movies can be traced back many centuries to the time of the ancient Greeks. They experimented with moving shadows, using lamps to make shadows on walls. Shadow puppets were developed, and they have been used to entertain people for hundreds of years. Then, in the 1660s, magic lanterns were introduced. These consisted of a lamp with a candle and a lens that could project pictures onto a wall. For many years, magic lanterns amazed audiences with pictures of characters from popular stories.

In the 1830s, toys that showed viewers sequences of still pictures in rapid succession were invented. The zoetrope, for example, consisted of a strip of paper with a series of small pictures on it, which was attached to a slotted drum. When the viewer moved the drum quickly and looked through the slots, the pictures appeared to move.

Optical illusions

All moving pictures are really optical illusions, which rely on the fact that the human brain retains an image for a fraction longer than it exists in reality. This means that if pictures are shown quickly enough one after the other, the brain is "tricked" into seeing a single unbroken movement. This is known as the "persistence of vision" theory.

Below **Each of these pictures is slightly different. When shown in rapid succession, they blend together, and the man appears to be walking.**

Capturing movement

New inventions in photography were also important in the development of movies. In 1889, the American inventor George Eastman developed the first roll of film made of celluloid, a transparent plastic. The glass and metal plates used by early photographers had to be replaced after each picture was taken, but with celluloid, pictures could be taken one after the other. It was a perfect system for recording moving images.

A few years later, a Scotsman named William Dickson invented the kinetoscope. This device projected perforated celluloid film at the rate of forty pictures per second—and the images appeared to move. The only drawback was that the kinetoscope could be viewed by only one person at a time.

The kinetoscope was the first machine to show moving pictures. Viewers peered down the eyepiece at the top to watch a show that lasted as long as twenty seconds.

NEW DEVELOPMENTS

The cinematograph allowed films to be shown to an audience for the first time.

Once inventors had discovered how to make pictures appear to move, they still had to find a way to project the pictures onto a screen so that more than one person could watch them at the same time. The problem was solved by the Lumière brothers in France in 1895. They developed a machine called the cinematograph, which recorded moving images and projected them onto a screen.

People were soon standing in long lines to see the cinematograph in action. The films that were shown were very short and featured events that today we would find rather boring—a baby being fed, for example. But the audiences of the time found these "movies" magical and amazing. An audience being shown a film of a train moving forward found it so realistic that they fled in terror!

Telling tales

Georges Méliès was the first person to show that film could be used to tell stories. From 1896, he based his films on fairy tales and science-fiction stories. They looked beautiful and included special effects to astonish audiences.

The "talkies"

Early full-length films had no sound tracks, although pianos or organs were sometimes used to provide music while the film was being shown. In 1927, the first talkie was released. Sound recorded on records was played at the same time as the moving pictures. For the first time, sound effects and the actors' voices could be heard.

Left **The first talkie was *The Jazz Singer*, starring Al Jolson. It was a great success.**

Below **The Technicolor three-color camera used red, green, and blue filters to record colors.**

Technicolor

In the early days of movies, only black-and-white films were shown. Color film could be produced only by tinting each frame by hand—a time-consuming process when you consider that there are twenty-four frames per second. The Technicolor process used a special camera, which photographed onto three strips of film instead of one. Each strip was sensitive to red, green, or blue. By combining these colors, the full range of colors could be made. By the 1950s, most movies were filmed in color.

THE MOVIEGOING EXPERIENCE

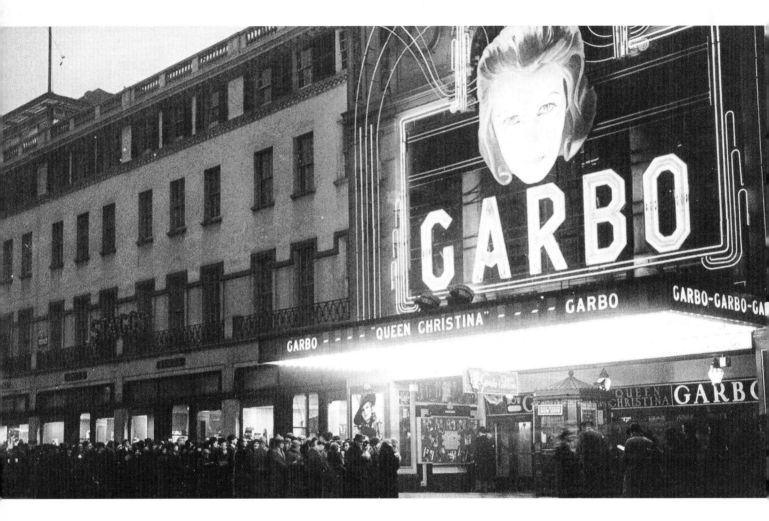

In the 1930s, audiences lined up around the block to see a movie. Here, people are waiting to see the Swedish star Greta Garbo in *Queen Christina.*

The U.S. film industry, which actually began on the east coast, started to flourish when studios were built in Hollywood, a small town in Southern California, in 1910. By the 1920s, more than 800 films were being made in Hollywood every year, and it had become the film capital of the world.

Moviegoing reached its peak during the 1930s and 1940s, when many people went to the movies at least once a week. In those days, theaters had restaurants, cafés, and even art galleries attached to them. Moviegoers would be greeted at the door by an attendant in full uniform and an usher would show them to their seats. While the crowd was waiting for the movie to begin, an organist would play. As well as being shown the main movie, audiences would also see a "B" movie—usually a mystery lasting about an hour—and a newsreel.

Fighting for survival

By the 1950s, movies were losing their appeal. Movie theaters were in need of repair, and ticket prices were rising. Television was becoming popular. It allowed people to watch "moving pictures" in the comfort of their own homes—and for free.

Movies tried to fight back with gimmicks that could not be found on TV. These included 3–D: audiences wore special cardboard glasses with different-colored lenses that appeared to make the images on screen come right up to them. Cinerama, which projected images onto three joined screens at the same time, also made audiences part of the action. Yet the number of people who went to the movies continued to decline.

Movies regain their popularity

In the mid 1970s, the situation began to improve. A group of talented young filmmakers, including George Lucas, Steven Spielberg, and Francis Ford Coppola, began creating films that earned such phenomenal amounts of money they were known as "blockbusters." Blockbuster films have sustained the movie industry to this day. Multiplex theaters—many screens available under one roof—replaced the now outmoded film palaces. Despite competition from videocassette recorders and cable networks, the film industry is booming once more.

THE TELEVISION AGE

Television broadcasting developed as a result of two important inventions. The first was cinema photography (see pages 6–8). The second was radio broadcasting: the technique of sending sound through the air, using radio waves.

Radio broadcasting

Radio broadcasting had been achieved for the first time in 1896, by the Italian scientist Guglielmo Marconi. He had figured out how to use radio waves to send messages over long distances. Once this breakthrough had been made, other scientists went on to discover how to capture pictures electronically and transmit these by radio waves.

Radio waves

Radio waves are invisible ripples of electric and magnetic force that travel through space at an incredible speed (a radio wave can go around the world seven times a second). They are just one of the many kinds of waves that make up the electromagnetic spectrum. Microwaves are also part of the electromagnetic spectrum, and they are used to send signals to and from communications satellites.

Radio waves look like the ripples in a pond when the surface is disturbed. The distance between the top of each wave is called the wavelength.

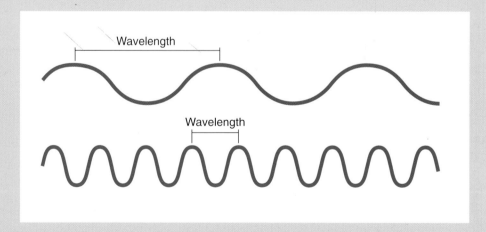

The number of waves that pass a fixed point in one second is called the frequency. In the diagram above, the lower wave has a shorter wavelength and a higher frequency than the upper one. Each radio station and television channel uses a different wavelength and frequency so that the signals do not get mixed up.

The invention of television

The first television set was developed in 1925 by a Scottish inventor named John Logie Baird. In the following year, he showed his television system to an audience and transmitted some fuzzy images. Other inventors, including Marconi, were also developing television equipment.

By 1929, few people owned television sets because they were still very expensive. But the number steadily increased, especially when model kits were developed so that people could make their own sets. At that time, television sets were about the size of modern portable televisions. The screen was much smaller than it is on modern televisions, and the reception was not as good as it is today. However, the fact that people could now receive moving images in their homes was amazing in itself.

History in the making: John Logie Baird demonstrates the world's first television system.

DEVELOPMENTS IN TELEVISION

The British Broadcasting Corporation (BBC) was the world's first television station. It began transmitting programs in 1932 but stopped just a few years later when World War II broke out. The United States did not start transmitting programs until 1939—but one year later there were twenty-three television channels on the air. The first programs were shown only in the early evening, and there were breaks between each program when nothing was shown at all. Television shows included plays, news, sports, and children's programs.

Technology surrounding television was diverted to the war effort, and it wasn't until the war ended in 1945 that attention was focused once more on television. In 1946 there were only 10,000 sets in the United States. By 1950 that number had jumped to 7 million, although even then broadcasting originated in just seven American cities, including New York, Chicago, and Los Angeles.

Behind the scenes: cameramen film a television program in the 1950s.

By the 1960s, many families owned color televisions. Eating habits changed, as people began to enjoy TV dinners in front of the set.

Bringing color into our lives

In 1954, the United States became the first country to show television programs in color, although color television was not widely available until the 1960s. Color television works in much the same way as black-and-white television. A television picture is made up of tiny dots. In color television, the dots are red, green, and blue instead of black and white. Different combinations of red, green, and blue dots produce the full range of colors when they are mixed together.

Video recording

The very first video system was invented by Logie Baird in the 1920s. It was developed further in 1956 and used by television companies to store programs before they were broadcast. Video recorders were not generally available to viewers at home until the 1980s. When people tape a program at home, their video recorder (VCR) picks up signals directly from their television aerial, satellite dish, or cable link and transfers them to the tape. Videotape is different from film: it is a magnetic tape, like those used to make sound recordings.

MAKING A MOVIE

Moviemaking today is a multi-million-dollar business, and people all over the world enjoy being entertained at movie theaters. Hollywood is still the center for making blockbuster movies, but filmmaking is also important in many other countries. India has a very successful film industry; more movies are produced each year in India than in Hollywood.

Film equipment

Although moviemaking has changed a great deal since the early days of cinema, the basic requirements—equipment to record the pictures and sound and to project the film for an audience—are just the same.

The film itself is made from a strip of photographic plastic called celluloid. The holes at the side of the film fit onto sprockets —toothed wheels on the movie camera and the projector—so the film can run smoothly.

A modern movie camera. The cameras used today look very different from those used by the first moviemakers, but the basic process of recording movies remains the same.

Feed reel
for film

Take-up reel
for film

Sprocket
holes

Film strip

Shutter

Diaphragm

Viewfinder

Light
source

Lens

Mirror

Inside a movie camera.
The diaphragm controls the
amount of light that reaches the
film while the shutter is open.
The mirror reflects light onto
the viewfinder.

How does the movie camera work?

A sprocket inside the camera holds the strip of film and pulls it
through the camera so that each frame stops exactly behind the
lens. When the frame is in position, a shutter moves out of the
way to let light reach the lens and film. A photograph is taken of
the scene that the camera can "see." Once the photograph has
been taken, the shutter drops back into place. This keeps any
more light from hitting the strip until the next frame moves
behind the lens. Today, most movie cameras take 24 pictures
like this every second.

Recording the sound

The sound for the movie is recorded by using a microphone on a
long arm known as a "boom." The boom operator has to make
sure that the microphone does not appear in the area that the
camera is filming. The sound is recorded onto a tape machine.
This is electronically controlled to ensure that the sound is
synchronized with the action being filmed by the camera.

BEHIND THE SCENES

Making a big-budget film requires a large number of people. As well as the actors, there are many people involved behind the scenes. Their work is needed to make the film a success.

The producer is in overall charge of the film from start to finish. He or she has to find a suitable script, hire the staff, obtain the money needed to make the film, and make sure everything runs on schedule.

Creating a "look"

The production designer is in charge of the overall "look" of the film and has to organize the design and building of the sets. The location manager looks for suitable places to film scenes that need to be shot outside the studio. If a castle is needed for a scene, for example, the location manager looks at various castles and takes photographs to show the director. Together, they agree on the most suitable location.

Hours of careful preparation are needed to create scenes that look dangerous and exciting on the screen. The set has to be safe for the actors and film crew to work on.

Filming a scene from *Speed*. The clapperboard is held in front of the camera to mark the beginning of each take.

Shooting the scenes

The director is in charge of filming. He or she makes decisions about how each scene should look and how the actors should deliver their lines. The director of photography works with the director, deciding on the camera angles, the lenses to be used, and the lighting, to ensure that the pictures the audience sees on the screen look perfect. The camera operator makes sure that each scene is in frame and in focus.

The clapperloader works as the camera operator's assistant, loading the film into the camera and sending it to be developed at the end of each day's filming. The clapperloader also writes the scene number and the take on the clapperboard at the beginning of each take and claps the clapperboard in front of the camera. This is so that each shot can be put together in the right order by the film editor.

Editing

Each scene is shot many times and from different angles. The film editor works with the director to put together the best takes to make the story of the film flow smoothly. The director looks at each take and decides which ones work best. The selected shots are then put together by the film editor.

PROJECTING A FILM

The projection room in the movie theater is the control center for everything that goes on in the auditorium. From here, the lights are dimmed, the music is played while the audience waits for the film to start, and the curtains are drawn. Most important, the film is projected from this room, through a small window at the back of the auditorium.

The projectors

The reels of film arrive in cans. Each reel lasts for about 20 minutes, so a film that lasts 100 minutes will use five reels.

Inside a film projector. Light from the powerful lamp inside the projector is directed onto the film strip by the condenser lenses.

A reel of film is placed in the projector spoolbox. The sprocket holes along the edges of the reel are held by the claws of the roller, in the same way as they are in the camera (see page 17). Like the camera, the projector pulls the film through at regular intervals. The difference is that when the shutter moves out of the way of the lens, a light inside the projector shines onto the frame that is in position. The picture that is on the frame is magnified and projected onto the screen in the auditorium. The shutter then covers the lens while a new frame slides into place. The images overlap at the rate of 24 frames per second to give the impression of a moving picture.

Feed reel for film

Powerful lamp

Shutter

Lens

Condenser lenses

Film strip

Take-up reel for film

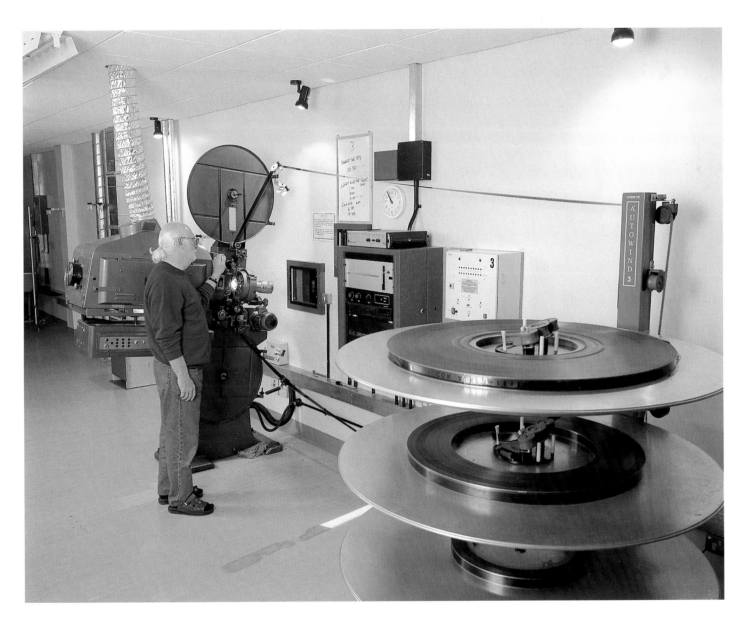

Picking up the sound

Each frame continues to the sound track reader. Here, a light shines through another lens (the optical head-reader) and onto a band on the side of the frame that carries the sound track. The information from the sound track is picked up and carried to a photoelectric cell that beams the sound to the loudspeakers in the auditorium.

The film then moves on to the take-up reel, where it ends its journey. This process is repeated for each reel of film.

The reels of film are fed through the projector by the projectionist. The film is projected onto the movie screen through the small square "window" in front of the projector.

TELEVISION PROGRAMS

In the control room, the director watches rows of screens. These display the shots taken by the cameras in the studio.

Many television programs are made in studios, and a television station usually contains several different sizes of studios. The studios contain the sets needed for the programs, with the background and props needed for each scene.

Television cameras

The television cameras are positioned in the studio. More than one camera is used, so the scene can be shot from different positions. These shots are mixed together, so that the viewer does not see the scene from just one angle. Television cameras work differently from film cameras because they do not carry film or videotape. Instead, they turn light into electric currents, or "picture signals." These signals are sent down a cable and are either broadcast live or recorded onto videotape so that they can be stored and transmitted later.

The production control room

The images from the cameras are displayed on screens in the production control room, where the director sits. He or she uses a microphone link to give instructions to the crew in the studio. They pick up the instructions through their headphones.

Outside broadcasts

News items and sports events have to be filmed outside the television station. These are known as outside broadcasts. A mobile control room is used as the production control room. The pictures from the cameras are sent there before being relayed to the television station.

Left **A folding satellite dish being carried in an outside broadcast unit.**

Vision and sound control

The picture signals from the cameras are sent down a cable to the vision control room. Here, the pictures are checked by the lighting director for brightness and by the vision controller for quality and color.

Microphones in the studio pick up sound from the scene that is being filmed and convert it into electronic signals. These are sent down a cable to the sound control room. Sound engineers check the sound quality and can change the volume and add music or special effects. The sound signals are then sent to the production control room and checked alongside the picture signals by the director.

A video editor at work. If a program is not going out live, it can be edited to make sure only the best parts are broadcast.

TRANSMISSION

TV signals

Television signals can be transmitted in either analog or digital form. In an analog signal, the information about how the sound and pictures are made up is transmitted in the form of electrical signals. In a digital signal, the sound and picture information is converted into a series of electronic digits. When the signal reaches the television set, the information is converted back into sounds and pictures by a decoder attached to the set. Sound and pictures transmitted digitally are of a better quality. Digital signals take up much less space than analog signals, so many more channels can be transmitted.

In the early days of television, all programs had to be broadcast live because the technology required to record them had not yet been developed. Today, most programs are prerecorded. This means that any mistakes can be taken out before the program is broadcast. Programs that are broadcast live are those where it is important to have the latest information, such as news programs or sports events.

Terrestrial broadcasting

The first stage in the process of getting television pictures to the viewers at home is called transmission. There are various ways in which this can be done. In terrestrial broadcasting, a transmitter at the television station combines the sound and picture signals of a program and converts them into radio waves. The radio waves are sent out from the transmitting mast at the station to transmitters around the country. These relay the signals to the aerials on people's homes.

The "forest of steel" near Albuquerque, New Mexico. These are the highest television antennas in the world.

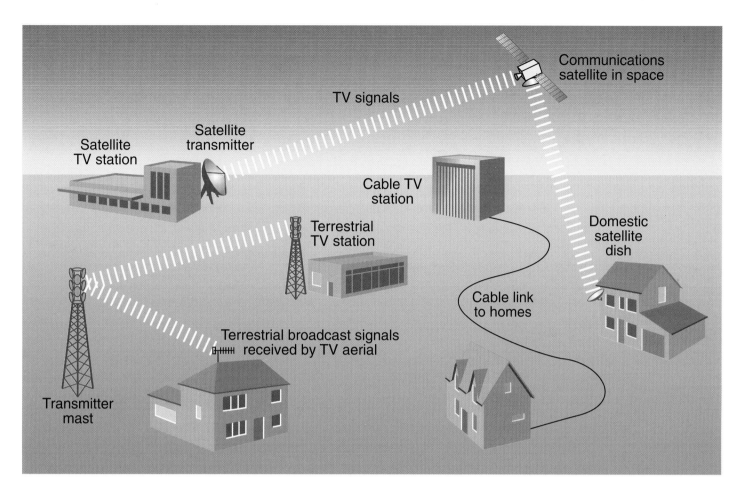

Programs can be transmitted by using transmitter masts, satellites, or cable links. Some homes are equipped to receive programs by more than one transmission method.

Transmission via satellite

The first program to be transmitted by satellite was broadcast in 1962. Sent from the United States to Europe, the program was received by 200 million viewers. Satellite transmission works by sending television signals in the form of microwaves into space from a large dish aerial. The signals bounce off orbiting satellites and are sent back down to Earth. Here, they are picked up by another powerful aerial, which relays them to a network of local transmitters. Alternatively, the signals can be sent directly from the satellite to small satellite receivers.

Cable television

Television signals can also be sent out through networks of underground cables. The signals are carried in the form of pulses of laser light, through fiberoptic cables. These are made of very fine threads of glass and can carry dozens of channels at a time. Once the signals reach people's homes, they are decoded by a device on top of the television set.

RECEIVING PROGRAMS

Television signals reach viewers' homes via an aerial, satellite dish, or cable. The signals travel along a wire into the television set. When the television is switched on, the sound and picture signals are separated. The sound is sent to the television's loudspeaker. The picture signal is sent to the cathode ray tube inside the set. Here, the signal is changed into the pictures that we see on the screen.

Making the picture

Inside the cathode ray tube, an electronic gun shoots the picture signals, in the form of beams of electricity, at the back of the screen. The screen is coated with a chemical that glows where the electric beams strike it. Each picture on screen is made up of hundreds of lines, which in turn are made up of thousands of dots. The electric beams scan back and forth across the screen 60 times per second. They strike the dots to make exactly the same pattern as the one picked up by the television camera when the program was filmed.

A magnifying glass looking inside a cathode ray tube. The magnets make the electric beams scan across the back of the screen in lines.

Electron guns

Electron beams

Magnets

Screen

Mask directs the beams as they scan across the screen

Magnified section showing glowing red, green and blue dots

A factory worker assembles televisions. The cathode ray tube can be seen in the center of each set.

Choosing a channel

There are many television channels to choose from, each showing different types of programs. The radio waves that carry terrestrial and satellite television signals are divided into channels, according to their wavelength and frequency. Each channel has room for only one station's signal. In cable television systems, the different channels are carried in the pulses of laser light in the fiberoptics.

Remote controls

When you press a button on the remote control, you are sending a pulsing beam of infrared light to a sensor inside the television set. The number of pulses will vary, depending on whether you want to adjust the volume or another control.

This viewer is using a remote control to lower the volume.

SPECIAL EFFECTS

By using special effects, filmmakers are able to turn fantasy into reality before our eyes. Special effects have been around since the earliest days of film—they were used by innovative filmmakers like Méliès, for example (see page 8). Sophisticated computer and film technology is used to produce special effects today, and this has had a tremendous impact on what we are able to see on screen.

Computer worlds

With the help of a computer, images can be altered in many different ways—by being squashed, moved around the screen, or split, for example. Computer-generated images can even be used to create the world in which the action takes place.

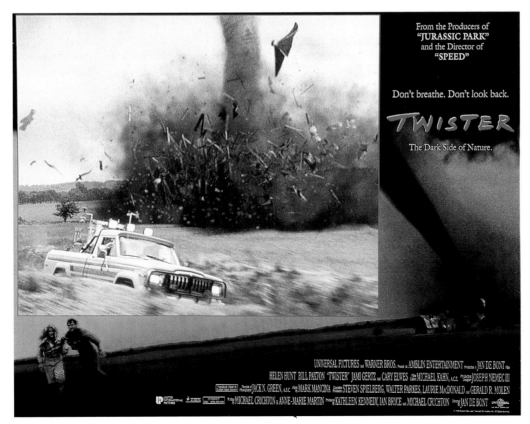

Examples of computer imagery can be seen in action films, such as *Twister*. In this film, the destructive tornadoes that provide the main storyline were created entirely on computer.

A poster advertising *Twister*. The tornadoes look terrifying, but they "exist" only within the computer.

Chroma-key

One of the most useful forms of special effect is called chroma-key—or blue screen. Imagine, for example, that a filmmaker wants to show someone traveling on a flying carpet. The actor sits on a carpet laid out on a blue bench against a blue background in the studio and pretends to fly. This is filmed, and the film is sent to the control room. Another film, showing the sky, is sent to a device called a switching board. Controls on the switching board direct the signals from the two films to combine together. Anything blue in the studio scene is made to disappear. This leaves a hole, into which film from the sky scene is inserted. The actor now appears to be flying on a magic carpet across the sky.

This technique can be used in many special-effects sequences. Weather forecasters can also do their reports in front of a blue screen—the map is added later, so the forecasters can only guess where they are pointing.

A scene from *Con Air*. The helicopter is being filmed in front of a blue background. These shots will be combined with a sky scene later, so that the helicopter appears to be flying.

ANIMATION

Animated films are probably the most popular form of entertainment for children today. The films of Walt Disney, for example, have attracted huge audiences for many years. Animation can be achieved in a variety of ways, and some films even combine animation and live action.

Cel animation

The earliest form of animation was achieved by photographing a sequence of drawings, each of which was slightly different from the one before. This kind of animation is still used today. The process begins with a series of pencil drawings, which are transferred onto sheets of transparent film called cels. These are sent to the camera department, where each one is laid over the background scenery and photographed—frame by frame. When 24 frames of animation are shown per second in film form, the drawings appear to move.

A scene from the Walt Disney film _Pocahontas._ Walt Disney's animated films are very popular and have taken in millions of dollars at the box office worldwide.

A scene from Nick Park's *The Wrong Trousers.* The film lasted approximately thirty minutes but took months of work to make.

Computer animation

New forms of animation include computer animation, as seen in films such as *Toy Story* and *Casper.* Images can be scanned into a computer or generated within the computer itself. Draco, the dragon seen in the film *Dragonheart,* started off as a wire-frame model, which was scanned into the computer. The dragon was then gradually built up using computer imagery and "brought to life." The images of the dragon were inserted into the scenes after filming had taken place. This means that, although on film the actors can be seen talking to Draco, they cannot actually see him.

Stop-motion animation

Stop-motion animation involves the filming of models or puppets. These are positioned and filmed for each shot before being moved slightly and filmed again. When the shots are put together, they give the appearance of movement. One of the best-known model animators is Nick Park of Aardman Animation. He has won Oscars, the most important awards in the film industry, for films starring the clay models Wallace and Grommit. Stop-motion animation involves a lot of time and effort. For the film *James and the Giant Peach,* only 45 seconds of the movie were completed each week.

USING FILM AND TELEVISION

People watch movies for many different reasons—to escape from reality into a fantasy world for a few hours, to marvel at the special effects, or simply to enjoy a good story. When people are asked why they watch television, they often mention the need to relax and unwind at the end of the day. As well as being entertaining, film and television can also be very useful in our daily lives.

Bringing people together

Television allows people to share the same experiences, although they may never meet. It can be a way of uniting the world and bringing people together on occasions of joy or sadness. The largest audience to date were the estimated 2.5 billion people worldwide who watched the live coverage of Princess Diana's funeral (in 100 languages) in September 1997.

A television camera films a tennis tournament. Television allows millions of people to share in the excitement of major sporting events.

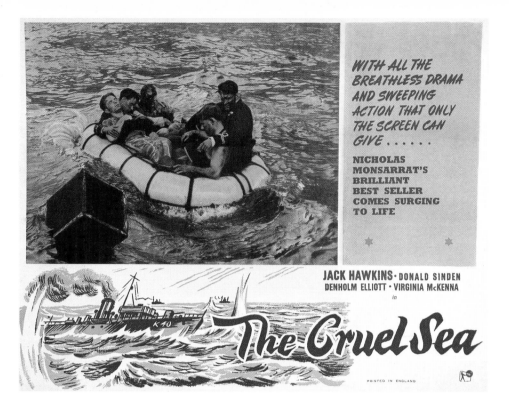

WITH ALL THE BREATHLESS DRAMA AND SWEEPING ACTION THAT ONLY THE SCREEN CAN GIVE . . . . .

NICHOLAS MONSARRAT'S BRILLIANT BEST SELLER COMES SURGING TO LIFE

JACK HAWKINS · DONALD SINDEN
DENHOLM ELLIOTT · VIRGINIA McKENNA
in

The Cruel Sea

PRINTED IN ENGLAND

Movies such as *The Cruel Sea* told stories of wartime courage. They were designed to inspire the audiences of the 1940s and 1950s, who might themselves one day be expected to show such courage.

Spreading information

Film and television can be educational. News and current-affairs programs, documentaries, and natural-history programs help people find out more about the world around them. Many people enjoy watching famous movies or television programs made in the past; this can help them understand why and how people in those times behaved as they did. However, it is important to remember that producers present information in a way that is interesting or exciting for their audiences. This sometimes means that facts are left out, altered, or made up, to create a better "story."

Propaganda

Before the age of television news, people used to see newsreels as part of a trip to the movies. During World Wars I and II, newsreels gave people vital information about how the wars were progressing. But the newsreels shown in Germany were very different from those shown in Allied countries. Each side would show its own version of events, emphasizing the successes and bravery of their own forces. The term for this is propaganda, and it describes the spreading of information that tries to persuade people to think in a certain way about an issue. Some governments today continue to use film and television as a way of spreading propaganda.

MARKET RESEARCH

A viewer makes a note of the program she is watching. The information she provides is used to help plan advertising and program schedules.

All sorts of companies use film and television to advertise their products to a large audience. Many television companies make money by selling time on screen to advertisers who run commercials during programs. Advertisers want to make sure that their commercials are being seen by the largest possible number of people. They also want to make sure that the people who are watching are those who are most likely to be interested in their products.

Checking the ratings

To find out how many people are watching the programs on each channel, ratings companies are employed. They work in two ways. One way is to choose a sample of people who represent the whole population. They are sent diaries in which they write down every program that they watch in a week. From this information, the total number of viewers for each program can be estimated.

Another method is to install meters on television sets in homes across the country. The meter has a button for each person in the family to press every time they start and stop watching television. The meter records not only what is watched, but also the age and sex of the viewer.

Although the information gathered by ratings companies is used mainly by program-makers and advertisers, it can also be useful in other ways. Sociologists, for example, would be interested in looking at the statistics, to see what they can learn about people's behavior.

Programs that appeal to children and teenagers are shown in the mornings on weekends.

Scheduling

Programs are carefully scheduled to appeal to the audience that is likely to be watching at a particular time of day. Children's programs are broadcast in the late afternoon, when the audience has come home from school. The biggest audiences watch in the evenings, when people are relaxing after a day at work. This is called "prime time." The programs shown in prime time, such as game shows and situation comedies (or sit-coms), are designed to appeal to as many viewers as possible.

TELEVISION AT WORK

Teletext

Certain stations broadcast a service called teletext. Viewers can obtain information by pressing numbers on their remote control. The information, which is put together on computer, appears in the form of text on the screen. The service is very useful for people wanting the very latest news—about the weather, sports results, business, or travel.

Operation TV

Televisions and video cameras are used in hospitals during certain operations. To find out what is inside a person's stomach, for example, a surgeon inserts an instrument called an endoscope. The fiberoptics in the instrument carry an image of the inside of the stomach back to the television screen, so that the surgeon can see what the problem is. An operation can be carried out using a laser beam carried by the endoscope.

Television screens are also used when pregnant women are given ultrasound scans—an image of the baby in the womb is transmitted to a screen, and the hospital staff can check that the baby is developing properly.

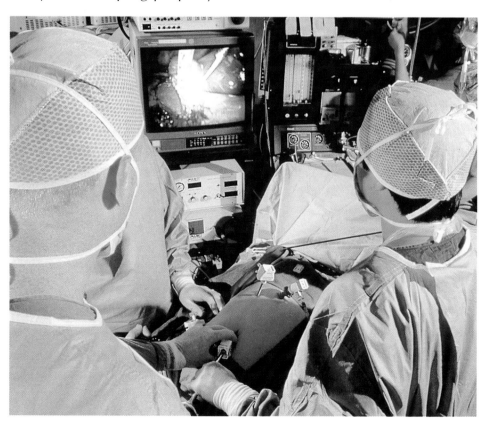

These surgeons are using an instrument containing a small camera to find out what is causing pain in a patient's stomach.

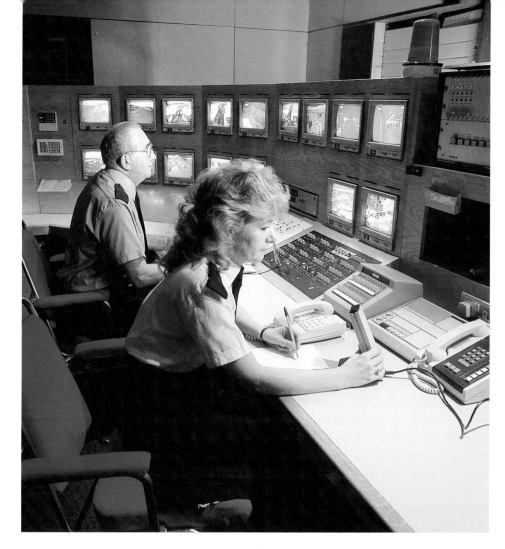

Left **Security officers keep an eye on what is happening outside the building by watching the screens. These display the images beamed in from video cameras.**

Below **Watch your speed! These roadside cameras photograph drivers who exceed the speed limit. The police can use the photographs as evidence.**

Television watchdogs

Security officers keep an eye on public places such as shopping centers, office buildings, banks, and bus and railroad stations, with the help of video cameras positioned around the buildings. The pictures taken by the cameras are monitored on screens at the control center. If security officers see a crime taking place, they can send someone to deal with it quickly. The videotaped pictures can also be used as evidence in court.

Television in traffic

Video cameras can be used to help control traffic. Pictures from cameras positioned near busy intersections are sent to traffic controllers, who can program traffic lights to help keep traffic moving smoothly. If the camera pictures show that there has been an accident or that some roads are very busy, the traffic controllers can warn drivers via travel news on the radio or by electronic signs along the highways.

THE FUTURE

All the developments described in this book have taken place in less than a hundred years. So what about the next hundred years? How will television and film develop in the future?

The digital future

In the past, equipment such as telephones, televisions, and computers all received signals and stored information in different formats—they could not "communicate" with each other. Using digital technology, information can be converted into a series of electronic digits, which can be read by many different kinds of communications equipment. Home computers can be linked to telephone lines and televisions.

Interactive television services will allow people to do their shopping without leaving home.

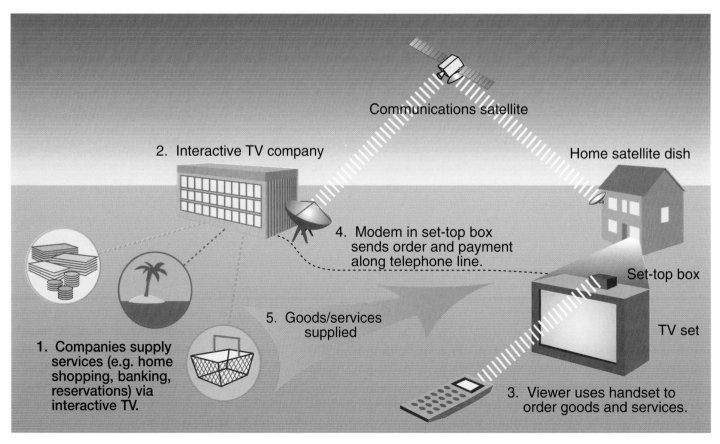

Communications satellite

2. Interactive TV company

Home satellite dish

4. Modem in set-top box sends order and payment along telephone line.

Set-top box

5. Goods/services supplied

TV set

1. Companies supply services (e.g. home shopping, banking, reservations) via interactive TV.

3. Viewer uses handset to order goods and services.

Hanging your TV

Scientists are working on a new flat television screen that can be hung like a painting. When the television is switched off, the screen could display images, such as works of art. A television like this would save space in the home because the screen could be hung on the wall. These new types of televisions could be ready for use in people's homes soon after 2000.

The same team of scientists is also developing screens that can be rolled up and carried around. This might be useful for soldiers, who could use the portable screens to display up-to-the-minute maps and information.

Left **A flat-screen television called the "Plasmatron." It is likely that we will all be watching televisions like this in the future.**

Soon, people will be able to look into events around the world by dialing live videos. With the right equipment, a person can already make a phone call and see the person he or she is talking to on a screen. This facility is useful for people at work, who can take part in meetings without having to sit together in the same room. It could also be useful for schools—pupils could take part in lessons, even though they are at home.

In the future, you will need just one machine for all of your communications. This device will receive television programs and will have split screens so you can see more than one program at the same time. Your machine will also act as a computer, accessing information from the Internet, and it will include a built-in video telephone.

CHANGING MOVIES

A movie audience enjoys the very latest in big-screen entertainment.

Once again, movies face a challenge from home entertainment. Since the 1980s, people have been able to watch videotapes of films at home. Today, they do not even need to visit a shop to rent or buy a video. Films are available on compact disc and can be downloaded from the Internet. People who own the equipment that is needed to select and watch the films can get a much wider choice, with higher-quality sound and pictures.

The big screen

Our visits to the movies are also changing. IMAX theaters show specially shot films on huge screens that are about 100 ft. (30 m) across and 78 ft. (24 m) high. Once the audience is seated, the screen completely fills their vision. The technique of 3–D movies, first introduced in the 1950s, may make a comeback. More realistic 3–D images projected toward the audience will make people feel that they are sitting in the middle of the action. They will not have to wear the special glasses that were needed in the past to experience the 3–D effect (see page 11).

The emaginator

Emaginator rides add a new element to the moviegoing experience and will soon be available in cities everywhere. People entering the theater are strapped into their seats and made to feel that they are traveling on the journey seen on screen, as their seats move up and down or side to side very quickly. The trips offered by the emaginator include a ride on a roller coaster, a trip down a mineshaft, and a flight to the moon. Soon, we will not just be going to the movies to watch a film but also traveling to places and dimensions never experienced before.

Step inside an emaginator and you may feel that you are actually experiencing the thrills of a roller coaster ride.

VIRTUAL REALITY

Virtual reality goes even further than 3–D movies. A film leads the viewer through a series of events created by the moviemakers, whereas virtual reality allows the user to interact with a computer-generated world. It is a bit like the difference between looking at a postcard and actually visiting the place. You can look at a postcard and wonder what the view would be like from a different point in the picture, but with virtual reality you can actually go and find out.

There are many ways of producing virtual reality. Some use headsets; others show a three-dimensional world on a flat computer screen. Many computer games use this system because it is a cheaper method than the headset system of producing a 3–D world.

The virtual-reality headset contains two TV screens providing stereo vision and headphones for stereo sound. The data glove and joystick allow the player to fire a "gun" at an opponent.

VRML

The computer language VRML (Virtual Reality Modeling Language) is used on the World Wide Web, which is part of the Internet. VRML allows three-dimensional worlds to be created, with which the users can interact.

In the United States, a computer network called Star Network allows children in hospitals around the country to interact with each other in virtual worlds generated by VRML. They can actually talk to each other and see a representation of the person to whom they are talking on the computer screen.

Virtual living

Soon, it will be possible for us to work, learn, shop, entertain ourselves, and communicate worldwide from the comfort of our own homes. For many people, this is an exciting prospect—but it could mean never meeting another human being face to face again. Still, film and television, together with other communications technology, offer us the opportunity to live in a completely new way.

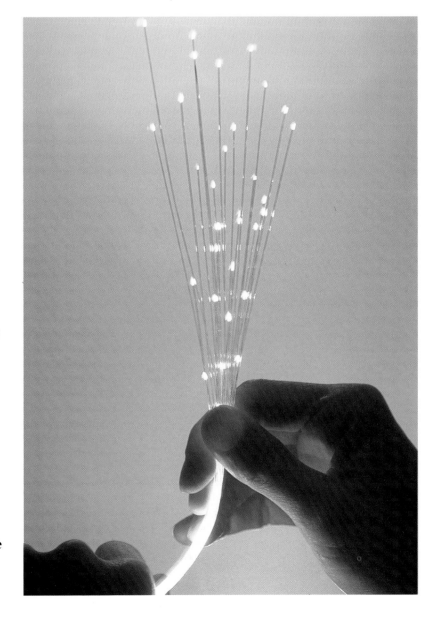

A fiberoptic cable. The hair-thin optical fibers are covered with plastic for protection. These small fibers of flexible glass represent the future of communications.

DATE CHART

1660s Magic lanterns are developed.

1830s The zoetrope is invented.

1888 The existence of electromagnetic waves is discovered by Heinrich Hertz.

1889 Celluloid film is invented by George Eastman.

1894 The kinetoscope is invented by William Dickson.

1895 The Lumière brothers present the first public film show, in Paris.

1896 Electromagnetic waves are used by Guglielmo Marconi to send messages —the world's first radio broadcast.

1905 Nickelodeons, the first movie theaters, are built in the United States.

1910 Hollywood begins to develop as the center for moviemaking in the United States.

1925 John Logie Baird develops the first black-and-white television set.

1927 The first talkie—*The Jazz Singer*—is released.

1928 A television set is installed in a home in the United States for the first time.

1932 The first regular television programs are broadcast from London by the BBC.

1941 The first television commercial is shown, in the United States.

1946 Sales of television sets boom after World War II. Stations begin broadcasting four or five times a week.

1950s Most movies are made in color.

1954 A color television system is developed in the United States.

1956 Videotape recording is introduced to store programs at television stations.

1960s Moviegoing declines as television takes over.

1966 Color television is widely available.

1969 Around the world, 700 million viewers watch television pictures of the first person to walk on the moon.

1970 The first IMAX films are released.

1975 Video recorders for use in the home are introduced.

1980s Multiplex movie theaters are built and audiences increase.

1990s The digital revolution begins, with access to the Internet becoming available to more and more people.

GLOSSARY

aerial The part of a television transmitter or receiver that sends or picks up signals.

animation The process of filming drawings or models one frame at a time, so that they appear to move when the film is run through a projector.

auditorium The area of a theater where the audience sits.

blockbuster A film that costs a lot of money to make, looks spectacular, and attracts large audiences.

communication satellite A machine that orbits the earth, receiving and passing on radio and TV signals.

control room A soundproof room that overlooks the set in a television studio.

digits Numerals. Only 0 and 1 are used in TV signals, in many different combinations.

edited Rearranged or shortened.

electromagnetic spectrum The range of different electromagnetic waves. Light waves, radio waves, and microwaves are part of the electromagnetic spectrum.

electromagnetic waves Invisible ripples of electric and magnetic force that travel through space.

fiberoptics Thin threads of glass or plastic through which light travels.

frame A single shot on a strip of film.

frequency The number of radio waves that pass a given point in one second.

infrared light A light that uses infrared waves, which have a longer wavelength than normal light waves.

interactive television A system that allows viewers to communicate with the TV screen.

Internet The world's biggest computer network, which allows people all over the world to share information.

laser A device that produces a narrow beam of light.

microwave A type of electromagnetic wave.

modem A device that passes information from a computer along a telephone line.

photoelectric cell A device that produces electric current when it is exposed to light.

project To throw the images from a film onto a screen.

reception Picking up the signals from transmitters.

script The story that is told in a film or TV program. It sets out the lines that the actors have to speak.

shutter The part of a camera or projector that opens to allow light to shine onto the film inside.

sound track The narrow band on one side of the film strip that contains all the sounds used in the film.

special effects Techniques used to create something that would be difficult or impossible to film in real life.

studio A soundproof room where films or television programs are produced.

takes Individual scenes, which may have to be filmed several times to make sure everything is just right.

3-D (three-dimensional) Appearing to have depth, so that on a film the action seems to come right up to the viewer.

transmission Sending out the electronic signals that carry television programs.

usher A worker in a movie theater who shows people to their seats.

wavelength The distance between the highest point of one radio wave and the next.

46

BOOKS TO READ

Cross, Robin. *A Behind the Scenes Look at Filmmaking*. New York: Sterling, 1995.

Cruise, Beth. *Behind the Scenes at "Saved By the Bell": An Inside Look at TV's Hottest Teen Show*. New York: Simon & Schuster Children's Books, 1992.

Gano, Lila. *Television: Electronic Pictures* (Encyclopedia of Discovery and Invention). San Diego: Lucent Books, 1990.

Hitzeroth, Deborah, and Sharon Heerboth. *Movies: The World on Film*. San Diego: Lucent Books, 1991.

Merbreier, Carter, and Linda C. Riley. *Television: What's Behind What You See*. New York: Farrar, Straus & Giroux, 1995.

Scott, Elaine. *From Microchips to Movie Stars: The Making of Super Mario Borthers*. New York: Morrow Junior Books, 1993.

Serrian, Michael. *Careers in Film* (Now Hiring). Parsippany, NJ: Silver Burdett Press, 1994.

Vitkus-Weeks, Jessica. *Careers in Television* (Now Hiring). Parsippany, NJ: Silver Burdett Press, 1994.

Wakin, Edward. *TV That Changed America's Mind*. New York: Lothrop Lee & Shepherd, 1995.

INDEX

Numbers in **bold** refer to illustrations